And see all the things
that a mouse can see

All things are bound together.
All things connect.
What happens to the earth
happens to the children of the earth.
Man has not woven the web of life.
He is but one thread.
Whatever he does to the web,
he does to himself.

Chief Seattle, 1855

Chief Seattle was a respected elder
of the Suwamish Indians in the
north-western United States, who
were forced into a reservation by
the white man about 135 years ago.
He made some notable statements
about the relationship between
man and nature, which still seem
important today.

DISCOVERING NATURE'S SECRETS

MARI FRIEND

NEW YORK   •   UNIVERSE   •   1992

for Kayleigh, Natalie and Daniel
with love from Grandma

Title page illustration:
solitary potter wasps fashion
thumb-nail-sized pots, using clay
moistened with water secreted from the
stomach. The wasp uses her mouth
and her front legs as tools.

Produced and designed by: SAVITRI BOOKS LTD
115 J Cleveland Street, London W1P 5PN, United Kingdom
Produced in Spain.

Published in the United States of America in 1992
by UNIVERSE
300 Park Avenue South, New York NY 10010

92 93 94 95 96 / 10 9 8 7 6 5 4 3 2 1

Library of Congress Cataloging-in-Publication Data

Friend, Mari
    Discovering nature's secrets: an all-year-round activity book/
Mari Friend.
        p.   cm.
    Summary: A collection of nature projects and activities, arranged
by the seasons, including raising butterflies, setting up an
aquarium, and observing life cycles of frogs and other aquatic
animals.
    ISBN 0-87663-638-5
    1. Nature study—Juvenile literature. 2. Natural history—Study
and teaching—Juvenile literature. [1. Nature Study. 2. Natural
history—Experiments. 3. Experiments. 4. Science projects.]
I. Title.
QH51.F75   1992
508—dc20   92-13166
                                                   CIP
                                                    AC

CONTENTS

DISCOVERING NATURE'S SECRETS

I have written this book to share with you my sense of wonder and enjoyment at the plants and animals I see around me and to encourage you to care for the environment in which we all live. There are suggestions for ways of observing small animals. There are games and other creative activities to stretch your imagination. The activities are set out season by season, but many of the projects can be carried out at any time during the year. Look for interesting things to do wherever this symbol appears.

Some of the activities take time and will need patience: raising butterflies and moths from caterpillars, watching tadpoles gradually change to frogs, and observing the lifecycles of simple aquatic animals cannot be done in a hurry. I have included clear instructions on setting up aquariums and on ways of feeding and caring for the small animals that you have chosen to keep for a while. Use kindness and respect when caring for animals and put them back into their natural habitat carefully as soon as you have finished observing them. The principle I advise you to follow when watching animals is, "Look with your eyes and not with your hands." Animals behave in a much more natural way—and live longer—if they are not handled more than necessary.

Even if you cannot visit the countryside very often, you probably have the opportunity to visit a park, and many of the trees, shrubs and animal tracks I have mentioned, can be found in parks.

Words appearing in **bold** in the text are explained in the glossary at the end of each section.

SPRING

Spring arrives when the lengthening days and the warmer sunshine encourage plants to grow. From early in the morning birds sing to proclaim their territories, and many other animals become active, for this is the beginning of a new year.

Frogs and toads abandon their winter hideouts and make for nearby ponds where they mate noisily and leave masses of frog spawn and strings of toad spawn. Male ducks in ponds and rivers begin to round up the females; scuffles break out with much quacking, while swans, moorhens and coots quietly build large, moundlike nests.

Mourning cloak and tortoiseshell butterflies leave the shelter of the plants and trees where they have spent the winter and, after warming their wing muscles in the sun, start to look for the food plants on which they will lay their eggs. Ladybirds begin their hunt for aphids; wasps rasp at fence posts to make wood pulp for nest-building; and bumblebees fly low in search of suitable nest holes. All of nature awakens.

Each animal prepares to raise a family when the particular food it eats becomes plentiful enough to meet the extra needs of giving birth and raising young. Frogs and toads lay their eggs early in the season, so that there is plenty of plant life for the tadpoles to eat when they hatch; but insect-eating tits and robins do not lay eggs until a month or two later, when the caterpillars they feed on can be collected from newly opened leaves. Birds of prey, such as kestrels, raise their young when there are plenty of mice and voles for them to eat; the mice and voles in their turn cannot feed their families until there are ample supplies of their particular food.

FOOD CHAINS

All plants and animals need food in order to live. In all the world of nature, only green plants are able to make their own energy-filled food. Green plants need mineral salts such as nitrogen, calcium and phosphates to help them to grow strong. They take in these salts, dissolved in water from the soil, through their roots, and a gas called carbon dioxide from the air through tiny holes known as pores in their leaves. Sunlight acts as the energy force that enables green plants to combine carbon dioxide and water to produce the basic food substances of carbohydrates and proteins. This process is called photosynthesis, which means "making things using light."

Animals are unable to make carbohydrates and proteins themselves. Some obtain their food directly from plants that grow in their habitat. Such animals are called **herbivores**. Sheep, cows and horses are herbivores. Can you think of other animals who eat plants?

Animals who feed on other animals are **carnivores**. Lions, otters and owls are carnivores. Many carnivores vary their diet and eat green plants and fruit as well as meat; these animals are called **omnivores**. Foxes, badgers and human animals are omnivores. Do you know the name that is given to people who do not eat meat? (You will find the answer on page 75.)

Carnivores are often called **predators** and the animals they feed on are called their prey. When a plant is eaten by a herbivore and the herbivore is eaten by a carnivore, the sequence of events is called a food chain. There are millions of three- or four-link food chains involving a plant, a herbivore and one or two carnivores. Here is a three-link food chain:

Grass is eaten by a rabbit and the rabbit is eaten by a fox.
No one eats the fox, so that is the end of the chain. The fox

is therefore the **top predator**. The chain is written down as:

grass ⟶ rabbit ⟶ fox

Foxes are particularly successful predators because they are opportunists—that is, they will eat almost anything they come across. Rabbits are only part of their diet: they will also eat other small mammals, birds, frogs and the contents of your garbage can.

Here is a four-link food chain:

A leaf is eaten by a caterpillar who is eaten by a small bird who is then eaten by a bird of prey who becomes the top predator, as no one eats him. Write it down as:

leaf ⟶ caterpillar ⟶ small bird ⟶ bird of prey

Can you think of any more three- and four-link food chains? (There are some suggestions on page 75.)

....

GLOSSARY **Carnivore:** a meat-eating animal e.g. a tiger.
Herbivore: a plant-eating animal e.g. a cow.
Omnivore: an animal who eats both plants and animals, e.g. a badger.
Habitat: the kind of place in which a plant or an animal lives e.g. a wood, the sea shore or a pond.
Predator: a hunting animal who captures prey.
Top predator: a predator who no other animal kills to eat.

A selection of 23 top predators, predators and their food.
Have fun getting to know them by playing the games
on pages 14 and 15.

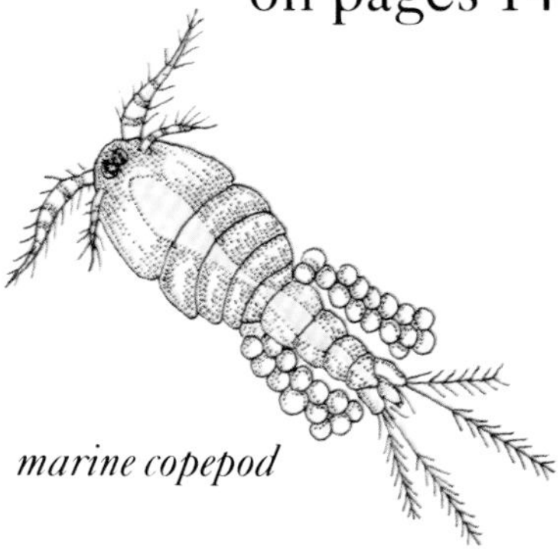

marine copepod

kestrel

cat

owl

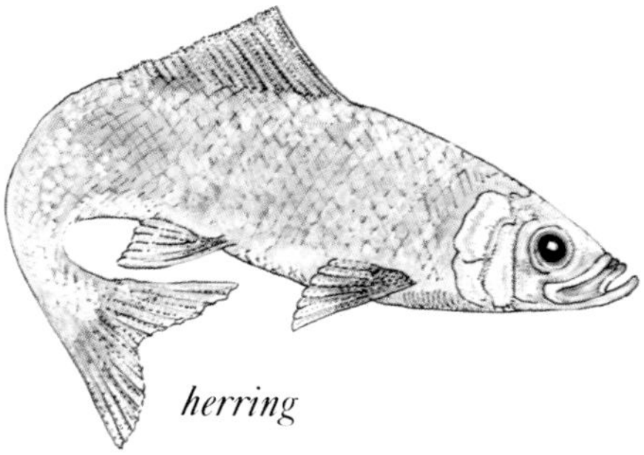

herring

small bird

weasel

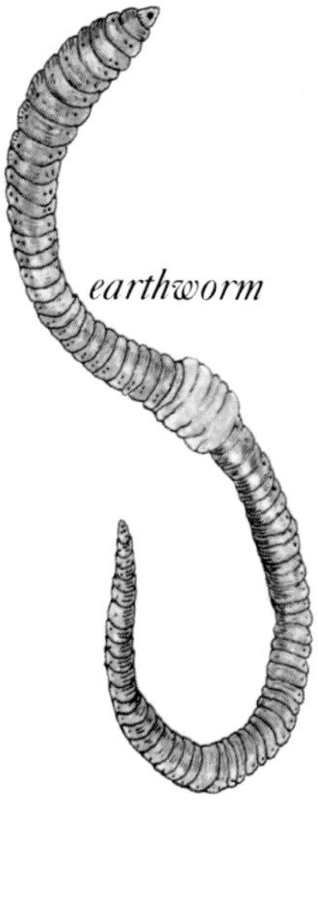

earthworm

rabbit

sand eel

wheat

field mouse

oak leaf

shrew

beetle

caterpillar

fox

diatoms and radiolarians
(microscopic marine plankton)

grass

common frog

herring gull

dung

leaf litter

You will need:
  a sheet of white card, at least 14 × 14 inches
  a few sheets of drawing paper
  a sheet of tracing paper and some glue (optional)
  pencil
  ruler
  scissors
  crayons or paints

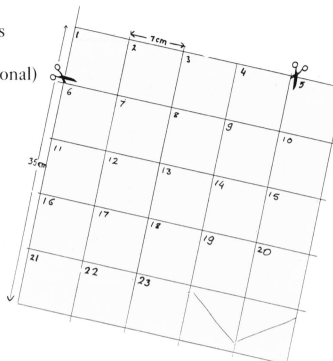

Measure the sheet of card out into
23 sections about 3 × 3 inches,
as shown on the right. Use the ruler
and the pencil to draw lines
to ensure that your cards are square.
Do not cut them yet.

Draw one of the animals or plants shown on pages 12 and 13 on to
each square, then color the pictures with crayons or paints.
If you prefer, you can trace the animals, using the tracing
paper. Cut out the drawings and stick them on to the squares. Use
crayons to color them, as paints do not stick to tracing paper.

Wait for the paint to dry and cut out your 23 cards.

Now arrange the cards into food chains. There are two
three-link chains, three four-link chains and one five-link chain.
Here is an example of a four-link chain to start you off:
the dung is eaten by the beetle, who is eaten by the frog, who is
eaten by the fox:

dung ⟶ beetle ⟶ frog ⟶ fox

Can you work out the other combinations? (There are some possible
answers on page 75, but try to work them out for yourselves.)

CREATING HABITATS

When you have finished making food chains, put the plants and animals into groups according to the type of habitat in which you could expect to find them: the oak leaf, the owl, the rabbit, the caterpillar and the fox in a wood, for instance.

Draw the habitat you like best on one of the sheets of paper and then turn the paper over and write an adventure story about the animals who live in that habitat and what happens to them.

PLAY THE MEMORY GAME

This game is to be played between two partners. You will need TWO sets of the cards you made for the Food Chain Game, in other words: 46 cards in all.

You will need: access to a photocopier; two sheets of white cardboard 14 × 14 inches in size; glue; scissors

The easiest way to make two new sets of cards is to arrange the first 12 of the original set, face down on to a photocopier. (12 cards will fit on to a sheet of A4 paper—four rows of three cards along the long dimension of the paper.) Make two photocopies. Position the 11 remaining cards. Make two photocopies.

Stick the four photocopied sheets on to the white card. The edges of the card should show on the photocopy; use these marks to help guide where to cut. You should now have 46 cards.

Mix the cards and spread them out face down. The two players take turns turning over two cards. When one partner finds a pair, he or she puts it to one side and goes again. If he or she does not find a pair, it is the other player's turn. At the end, the player with most pairs wins.

FOOD PYRAMIDS

A food pyramid is made up
of very many plants which are
eaten by many plant-eaters.
The plant-eaters are eaten by fewer
flesh-eaters, who are eaten by a very few
top carnivores who have no predators other than man.
So you have a pyramid of numbers.

The food pyramid on this page shows five food chains.
Follow the tracks to find out which predator eats what.
For example, hawthorn berries   are eaten by a mouse,
who is eaten by an owl —   the top predator.

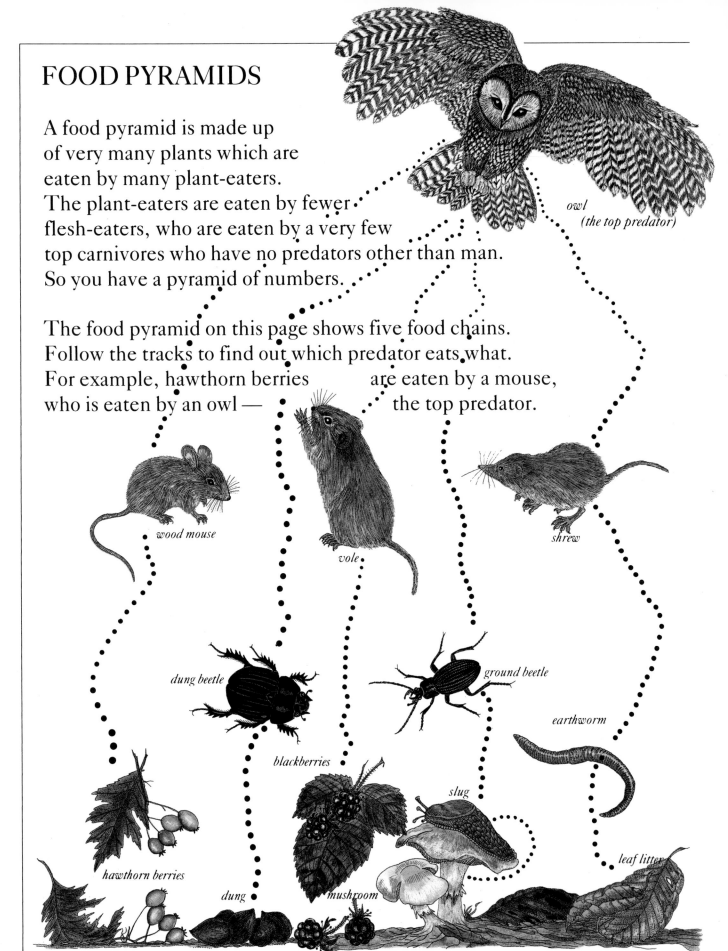

owl
(the top predator)

wood mouse

vole

shrew

dung beetle

ground beetle

earthworm

blackberries

slug

hawthorn berries

dung

mushroom

leaf litter

Now that you have got the idea, read the food chains in the way they are usually written:

blackberries → vole → owl
mushroom → slug → ground beetle → owl
leaf litter → earthworm → shrew → owl

Which food chain is missing?

★ HAVE FUN MAKING A MOBILE

You will need:
  a metal coathanger
  a sewing needle
  some black cotton
  a piece of thin cardboard or stiff paper
  tracing paper
  a pencil
  some paints or felt-tipped pens
  a pair of scissors

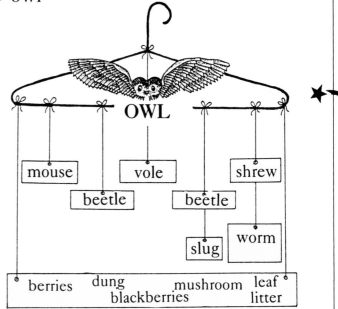

*This mobile illustrates
the food pyramid shown opposite.*

To make your mobile, draw any top predator or carnivore, such as a fox, a lion or a human being, then add the animals this predator eats and the food that is eaten by those animals. You may prefer to trace off the animals and plants that I have drawn, enlarging them on a photocopier at school. I used a tawny owl as the top predator in the mobile I made. An owl is a **bird of prey** who eats small **mammals** such as mice, shrews and voles, and they eat the food that is pictured below them.

Draw the plants in a strip that is the same width as the coathanger and about 2 inches deep. Draw the animals and color them in before cutting them out carefully with the scissors. It is a good idea to color both sides of the card shapes, as they will twist around in a draught, showing both sides of each picture.

Using the needle, thread a length of cotton through the top of each animal shape. Suspend the bird of prey from the bottom of the hook of the coathanger, so that it hangs above the rest. Now hang the birds or mammals whom the bird of prey eats from short threads tied along the bottom bar of the hanger.

Fasten the smaller creatures these birds or mammals may eat on longer threads so that they hang below their predators. Finish your mobile off by suspending the strip of plants, fastening it to the bottom bar of the coathanger by a thread at each end of the strip. The plant strip will hang below everything else and will balance the mobile well when you finally hang it up.

If you would rather make a poster, then you could give your food pyramid a background of trees, houses or grasses drawn in silhouette (a shape colored in black). For example, the owl food pyramid on page 16 could have a background of dark tree shapes and a crescent moon.

GLOSSARY   **Bird of prey:** a bird which kills and eats other birds and mammals. Its hooked beak and strong feet with four sharp claws are designed for holding and tearing prey.
Mammal: a class of animals whose young are fed on milk from their mothers' bodies.

FOOD WEBS

Some animals have a variety of food sources and may also be eaten by several different predators. This allows the animals to survive if their main food becomes scarce: for example, the diet of a fox or a badger includes earthworms, beetles, slugs, snails, grubs and berries. This food will also be eaten by birds and small mammals, and all but the berries will be hunted and eaten by snakes, lizards, frogs, toads and newts.

Food chains therefore criss-cross with one another to make a food web. Food webs occur in almost every habitat; here we will think about the food web in a freshwater pond. When you visit a pond, take an adult with you if possible.

IF YOU GO ON YOUR OWN, TELL AN ADULT WHERE YOU ARE GOING, AND STAY AWAY FROM DEEP WATER AND DANGEROUS PLACES.

In a freshwater pond there are **algae**, as well as many plants so small that they can only be seen through a microscope. These minute plants (along with **microscopic** creatures and **organic** debris) are eaten by tiny animals such as water fleas and cyclops, which are in turn eaten by many members of the pond community, including tadpoles, water beetles, newts and small fish. These predators are then preyed upon by larger fish and by water birds; large fish and ducks may be eaten by man.

....

GLOSSARY   **Microscopic:** too small to be seen except through the lens of a microscope.

Algae: plants of the seaweed family, found in (singular **alga**) seas, fresh water and damp places.

Detritus: fragments of stones, silt and debris such as may be found at the bottom of a pond.

Organic: to do with, or derived from, living plants or animals. "Organic" food is food grown without using chemical, inorganic fertilizer.

You will need:

tracing paper	paints or crayons
drawing paper	scissors
pencil	glue

Trace off, or copy, the animals on the right and the pond picture below. Color them and cut them out carefully.

perch

Now put the animals on to the pond picture, in the areas in which you would expect to find them. For example, the tubifex worm is usually found at the bottom of the pond among the **detritus**. There is a guide on page 75. Make sure the animals are correctly placed, then stick them down on to the picture.

tadpole

moth larva

diving beetle

water boatman

cyclops (freshwater copepod)

water scorpion

daphnia

mayfly nymph

water snail

midge larva

tubifex worm

dragonfly nymph

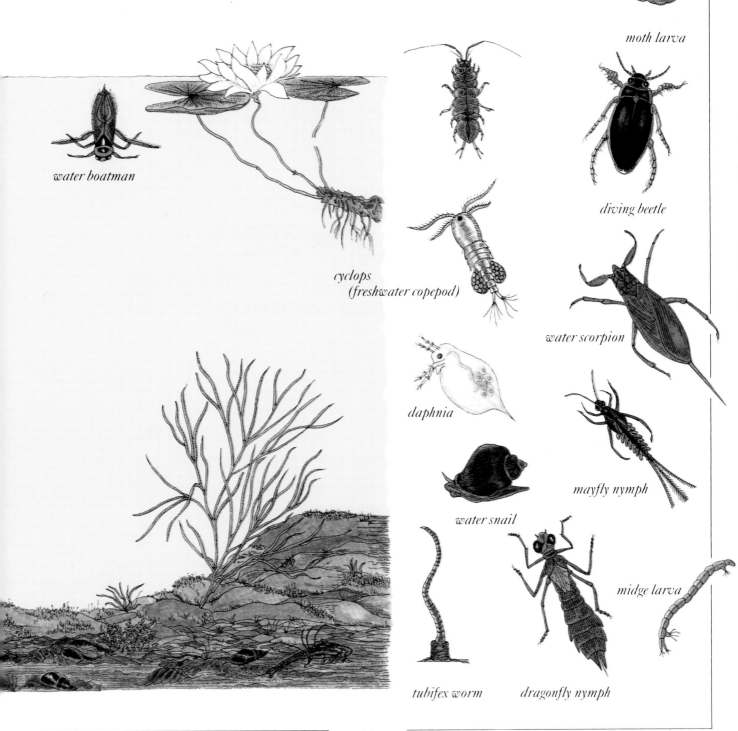

A TEMPORARY HABITAT IN AN AQUARIUM

Why not try "dipping" a few animals from a pond and keeping them for a short time in habitats of your own creation? Do not forget that the animals that you keep are totally at your mercy. Because of the delicate nature of this activity we suggest that it be supervised by an adult. When taking creatures out of their own environment we must do it sensitively and responsibly. Your family or your class at school could join in, for example. Do not be put off by the advice that follows. It is based on personal experience and could prevent the loss of the contents of your aquarium. It is most important to keep everything clean, including your hands. It is not necessary to have a large tank or a pump for aeration unless the animals normally live in fast-moving water.

Your animals will need feeding very often during spring and summer; think about this carefully BEFORE you begin to keep animals in your tank. Many aquarium shops sell live daphnia and bloodworms, or you may know a pond or a water butt where you can collect midge **larvae**. These are ideal for feeding fish, carnivorous insects and tadpoles.

A clear-sided tank is ideal: clean and rinse it thoroughly. Make sure you have an adult to help you. Gravel bought from a pet shop makes the best base for the habitat; builders' sand or soil becomes stale very quickly and the water doesn't clear. Wash the gravel under a running tap until the water runs clean.

Slope the gravel from the back of the tank toward the front so that there is at least 1 inch at the front and twice this depth at the back. This ensures that debris will mostly collect at the front; you can then remove it using a siphon, but be carful: siphons have a nasty habit of sucking up little animals too! As an alternative, introduce bloodworms; they feed on waste and will do the cleaning in a well-balanced tank.

Use well-scrubbed and scalded rocks or large stones from the garden to create a background with plenty of hiding places. TAKE CARE WHEN USING HOT OR BOILING WATER or let an adult do it.

pondweed with snails' eggs

Wash water plants well and remove any dead leaves. Are there any jelly-covered batches of snails' eggs on the leaves? A few snails are useful as they eat algae from the sides of the tank. Push the base of the plant stems sideways into the gravel and anchor them with a large stone. Plants produce oxygen in daylight, but use oxygen and produce carbon dioxide in darkness. Too many plants will make it difficult for the animals, who need oxygen to breathe at night.

Before filling the tank make sure that it is not standing in full sunshine, as the sun will warm the water and kill the animals. Add the water and gently, using a jug or a jar, pour it on to one of the rocks so that the gravel and the plants remain undisturbed. Leave the tank to stand overnight.

When you introduce animals to your tank, try to make sure that the temperature of the water they are entering is similar to that which they are leaving. Lower the animals into the water carefully; do not allow them to fall into the water.

Tapping on the sides of the tanks sends shock waves through the water and hurts the animals. DO NOT DO IT.

Before you put other animals into an established tank, beware of overcrowding and of putting predators in with prey or vice versa; for example, if you put a dragonfly **nymph** in with your tadpoles you will soon have a fat nymph and no tadpoles. It is as well to keep dragonfly nymphs and diving beetles in tanks of their own with only food and snails for company.

dragonfly nymph

Diving beetles will fly and water striders will climb out of a tank unless gauze or very fine curtaining is tied over the top.

Leave tap water to stand overnight before adding it to your tank. Dust will settle on the surface of the water in the tank; this can be scooped off with a jar and carefully replaced with fresh water.

In warm weather the water in the tanks will quickly become stale, but this can be controlled by ladling out about half the water and replacing it gently with water that has been standing.

When you have finished observing the animals, return them to the pond: dip the container below the surface of the water and allow the animals to swim away.

diving beetles chasing a tadpole.

ALTERNATIVES TO TANKS

If you haven't got a tank or the feeding of the animals worries you, try raising small insects in a large jar or bowl. Midge larvae may not sound very exciting, but their life cycle is interesting. You can raise snails from eggs and observe their adult behavior in a small container. One or two caddis larvae can be kept in a large jar. (Discover their life cycles on page 26.) Mayfly nymphs do not need a great deal of space either. Keep the animal numbers low and you will be able to watch plenty of action in miniature.

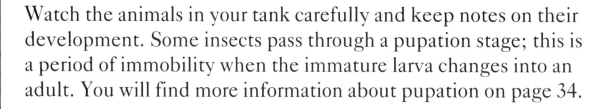

mayfly nymph

Watch the animals in your tank carefully and keep notes on their development. Some insects pass through a pupation stage; this is a period of immobility when the immature larva changes into an adult. You will find more information about pupation on page 34.

Watch for the stages:

egg • larva • pupa • adult

This is called complete **metamorphosis**.

Some insects do not have a resting stage; instead they gradually change into an adult. As these insects grow, they have to shed their skin, because it will not stretch; each time a skin is shed the larva is one step nearer to becoming an adult. The number of skins the insect must shed varies from species to species. These immature insects are usually called nymphs and their development is called incomplete metamorphosis.

The stages are:

egg • nymph • adult

Put the animals back into their own habitat carefully when you have finished watching their development.

....

GLOSSARY **Nymph:** the name given to the young stages of those insects which gradually change into adults.
Larva: the name given to a young insect when it (plural **larvae**) is markedly different from the adult, e.g. a caterpillar.
Metamorphosis: the changes that take place in an animal's life as it turns into an adult.

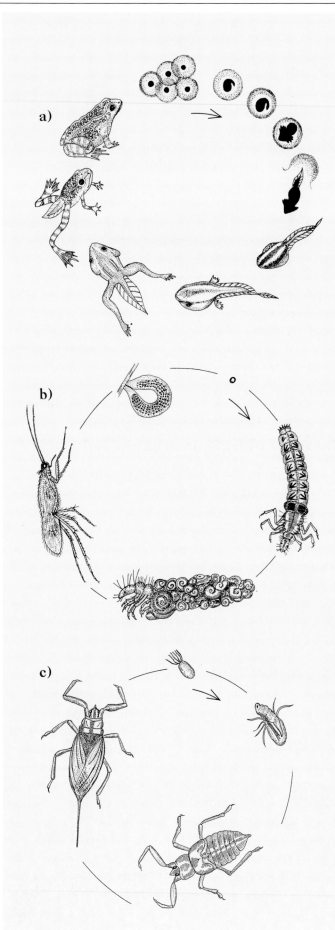

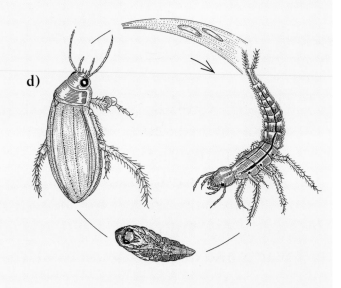

a) You will find masses of frog spawn in some freshwater ponds in early spring. The tadpoles hatch in 10 to fourteen days and complete their metamorphosis in about three months. Tiny froglets must be allowed to leave the water or they drown.

b) Caddisflies of still water lay their eggs in masses on water plants. The vegetarian larva makes itself a characteristic protective case. The larval period lasts about a year and pupation—spent in the case—takes several weeks.

c) If you catch a water scorpion, it will pretend to be dead. It lays its eggs individually on plants just below the surface of the water. The nymphs have a very short breathing tube and no wings; they do not pupate but develop gradually to the adult stage.

d) Diving beetles lay their eggs into the stems of plants. Keep only two or three larvae in a small tank. When the larvae are ready to pupate they must be able to leave the water or they will drown, so when they are well grown, slope the tank by putting a wedge under it at one end. Make a bank at the shallow end using sphagnum moss (available from a garden centre or a florist). The larvae will then be able to climb out of the water.

# SUMMER

Gradually spring turns into summer, bringing long days of hot sunshine and short, warm nights. This is the season when many animals raise their young—not only because food is readily available and the long hours of daylight give extended time for hunting, but also because the lush plant growth offers protection from predators. The season of plenty is short, so plants and animals must make the most of it.

By day, colorful flowers attract bees, butterflies, hoverflies and beetles to their stores of nectar and pollen, while fragrant blooms of almost luminous white, mauve and pale yellow invite moths to visit them by night. Caterpillars munch leaves and in their turn are collected by birds who have hungry young to feed. By midsummer most of the surviving caterpillars have gone into pupation and the birds turn their attention to the increasing numbers of flying insects.

Many birds spend their summers in North America because the favorable conditions mean there is a feast of insects. Warblers, flycatchers, swifts, swallows and martins are among the birds who arrive here from Tropical America to raise their families, completing their migration with the return flight in the autumn.

The frantic food-gathering activity of birds and small mammals makes them vulnerable to their predators. Birds of prey, weasels, foxes, cats and many other hunters wait to pounce on tired individuals and inexperienced young; there are food chains wherever you look at this time of the year.

LIFE IN A POND

The following projects look at some of the interesting creatures which live in the pond. Remember: WATER IS DANGEROUS. When you visit a pond, ask an adult to go with you; if you must go on your own, take great care and ALWAYS TELL AN ADULT WHERE YOU ARE GOING.

Examine the top of the pond for insects who walk on the surface of the water. These creatures, water striders for instance, weigh very little. Instead of having a claw on the tip of each foot as most insects do, they have water-resistant hairs enabling them to walk on the surface which is like a tightly stretched elastic skin. This project shows you how it works:

 ## WALKING ON THE WATER

You will need: a shallow bowl; a small piece of blotting paper; a sewing needle

Fill the bowl with water; float the piece of blotting paper on the surface and carefully place the needle on the paper. It will soak up water and sink, leaving the needle floating on the surface. Try floating the needle without using paper.

 ## BREATHING IN MUDDY WATERS

You will need: a clean jelly jar; a fine-meshed pond net; a magnifying glass

Rat-tailed maggot

Using the net, catch a rat-tailed maggot in the mud at the edge of the pond. Put it into the jar with a little water. Its "tail" is in fact a breathing **siphon**. With the help of the magnifying glass, watch it extend through the water surface. If you add a little water, the siphon will increase in length.

GLOSSARY   **siphon:** some water-dwelling animals have a tubelike extension to their body that enables them to breathe in air.

GARDENING FOR WILDLIFE

The world of wildlife begins just outside your door—whether you have a large garden or a small one, a backyard with flowerpots or just a bare brick wall.

If you have a patch of garden to yourself, you could make it into a mini-nature reserve. Grow flowers to attract bees and butterflies; other insects will then come to feed on leaves or sap. Birds will arrive to feed on the insects, and on any seeds and berries in the garden.

The picture opposite shows nine habitats, any one of which you could create in your garden. A pond attracts many animals, including frogs, toads and dragonflies, and it is fascinating to watch. Many creepy-crawlies hide in leaf litter and in a dry stone wall—or even in a pile of large stones. Who will come along to hunt them out? Who else will make a home in an old wall? You will find some answers on page 75.

Wild flowers can be grown from seed; remember that weeds too are flowers that attract many insects. Some fruiting trees and shrubs can be grown from cuttings —a gardener will show you how— then birds will come to eat the fruits and berries. Why not feed the birds regularly on a bird-table, putting the table where cats cannot jump on to the birds? A few logs in a pile will provide a damp refuge in a shady place, while in the sun some loose

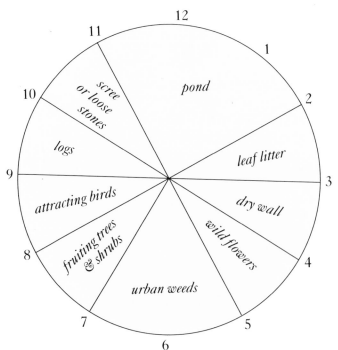

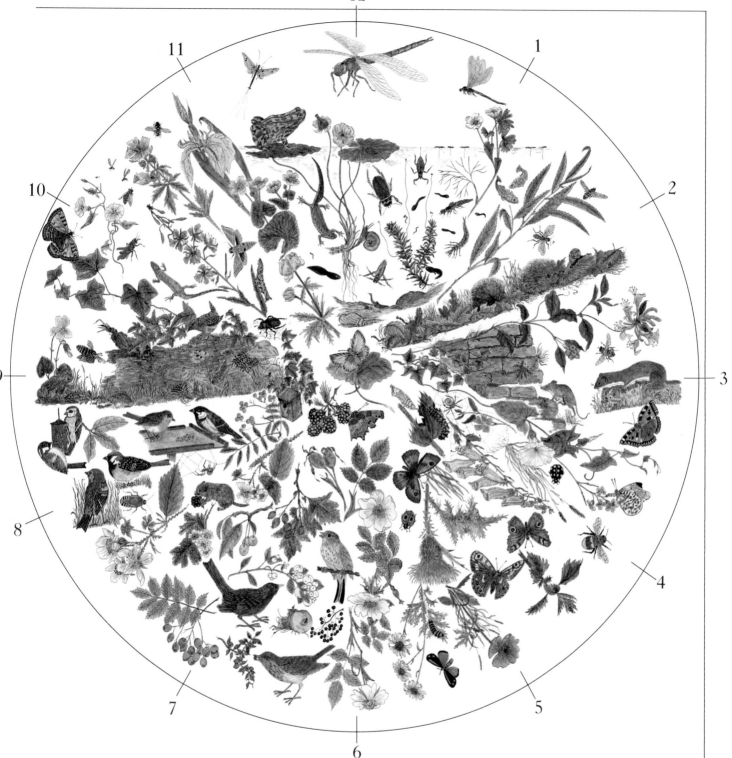

stones on a sandy bed (scree) will create a warm spot on which
lizards, butterflies and moths can sun themselves.

If you haven't got a garden, then grow flowers in window-boxes,
hanging baskets or containers. You will be surprised at the
number of small animals these simple habitats will attract.

This is a corner of my wild garden. In this small area there are 20 plants and 24 animals. See how many you can find.

BUTTERFLIES AND MOTHS

A typical caterpillar

Some caterpillars are easy to look after. REMEMBER
to keep their containers clean, well supplied
with fresh food, and out of direct sunlight.

Butterfly or caterpillar cages can be bought; or you could make
one yourself. Do this BEFORE you start collecting caterpillars.

★ BUILDING A CAGE AND RAISING CATERPILLARS

You will need:
>   an old, round cake tin
>   a sheet of acetate
>   a hammer and a nail—WITH PERMISSION FROM AN ADULT
>   a small bottle which will fit inside the finished cage
>   some cotton wool

*A caterpillar cage can be bought
or made, as explained.*

Make some airholes in the cake tin lid by putting the lid flat
side down on to a scrap of wood and knocking the nail through the
lid with the hammer. This is a quick, neat way to create holes
in plastic or tin. Bend the acetate into a tube that will stand
in the cake-tin bottom and fix the edges together with sticky
tape. Fit the lid on top and there is your caterpillar cage.

Collect some caterpillars, leaving them on the leaves of the
plant they were feeding on to avoid touching them. Find out the
name of the plant, as the caterpillars may not eat anything else.
Stand the plant pieces in the small bottle of water. Use cotton
wool to seal the top and prevent the caterpillars from drowning.
Stand the bottle inside the cage. The caterpillars eat quickly.
Put new food stems in amongst the old; the leaves must be dry. As
the caterpillars move on to the new food, take away the old; if
you must move the caterpillars, use a paint-brush to lift them.
Clean out the droppings every day, as they soon become moldy.

CHANGING SHAPE

All caterpillars will stop feeding when they become
too fat for their skin; then you may see them wriggle
out of the skin and begin to feed again.

caterpillar
a)

b)

c)

d)
pupa

When the caterpillar is fully grown it begins to look around for a
suitable place to **pupate**. Many butterfly caterpillars will pupate
hanging from the lid of their cage or from the stems of their food
plant; you could give them some thin twigs to hang from. Some
butterfly and many moth caterpillars prefer to pupate in a silken
cocoon in soil; so when your moth caterpillars begin to look big
and fat put about 2 inches of soil in the bottom of their container.

The caterpillar then sheds its final skin and enters the **pupa**
or chrysalis stage. The word "pupa" is Latin for doll or
puppet and many moth pupae do look like a doll wrapped in a
shawl. "Chrysalis" is from a Greek word meaning gold and
refers to the shiny spots which can be seen on the papery cases
of some pupating butterflies.

When the caterpillar has gone into **pupation** it begins to
dissolve, leaving the pupa case filled with fluid. Gradually a
butterfly or moth begins to take shape inside, developing from
special little groups of cells. Soon the shape of the adult insect
can be seen through the pupa case, and one day the case breaks
and out comes the winged insect in all its glory.

egg

This process may take weeks or months—and
the emperor moth caterpillar may take up to
two years—but it is a wonderful thing to watch.

pupa case

butterfly

larva

*The life cycle of a
red admiral butterfly.*

Release the adult butterflies into the sunshine
and put moths into a shady bush; soon they
will lay eggs and you can start all over again.

To the non-scientist, there is no clear distinction between butterflies and moths, except that all butterflies fly by day. They have clubbed antennae ("feelers" with knobs on) and most have brightly colored wings. Butterflies usually fold their wings together when they are at rest, while moths tend to rest with their wings flattened downwards, like a sloping roof.

Some moths are also bright in color and active by day, but most have dull-coloured wings and fly by night. Moth antennae vary from being thread-like to resembling tiny feathery plumes.

The project on page 36 will help you to discover the colors butterflies like best.

butterfly

butterfly

butterfly

moth

moth

butterfly

butterfly

butterfly

moth

butterfly

moth

butterfly

WHAT COLOR DOES A BUTTERFLY LIKE BEST?

Choose a still, sunny day for this project.

You will need:
a tray
4 saucers
sugar, glucose or honey
dissolved in water to make a syrup
enough thin white cardboard to cover the 4 saucers
pencil and scissors; paints or crayons

Put the saucers face down on the cardboard. Trace around them with a pencil. Cut out the circles. Place a quarter in the center, draw around it and cut it out. Draw a simple flower shape, as shown above, and cut it out. Color the petals brightly, making a blue, a red, a white and a yellow flower.

Put the saucers on the tray and place everything close to a flowerbed. Pour a little of the syrup on to each saucer and cover each saucer with a paper flower. Sit quietly some short distance from the tray and watch who comes to investigate the heart of your "flowers". Which color do they prefer?

GLOSSARY   **Pupa:** the third stage (after egg and larva) in the life of insects, such as butterflies, whose shape changes completely between immaturity and adulthood.

Pupate: to become a pupa.

Pupation: the state of being a pupa.

Cocoon: a case which protects the pupa of many insects, especially moths. It is made of a tightly wound thread spun by the larva before it pupates. The cocoons of silk worms are used to produce silk.

HEDGE PLANTS AND INSECTS

Hedges are the bushy borders which separate one field from another. They form one of the most varied habitats for plant and animal life as well as being a useful boundary to a piece of land. Farm animals can be safely enclosed by a hedge, which also provides them with shelter from rain and snow. Hedges form a windbreak for crops, preventing valuable topsoil from being blown away. A hedge bordering a field often has a ditch that carries away surplus water from the soil, making the ground easier to work.

A typical hedge is made up of shrubs entangled with brambles, ivy and other climbing plants. This habitat is a haven for insects and spiders, and an excellent place for birds to nest and feed. Small mammals live along the hedge-bank, while frogs and newts enjoy the dampness of the ditch. In turn, all the animals living along a hedge attract the predators who hunt them.

Many flowering plants grow on the hedge-bank. Some enjoy the shade, some the sun; some like the soil to be moist, while others thrive in a dry, sandy soil. Look at a hedge near you at different times of the year; make a list of the plants that grow there. What insects visit the plants? Which birds nest there in spring? Have you seen any mammals there or found their tracks or trails (see pages 62–67)? Can you make some hedge food chains?

Plants growing by the roadside are often cut back to improve visibility for motorists. Or they may be sprayed with herbicides, which are chemicals designed to kill unwanted plants. What effects do you think this has on the animals who live in the hedge or who visit the flowers?

Do you think it is a good idea to kill the plants, or would it be better to cut them back?

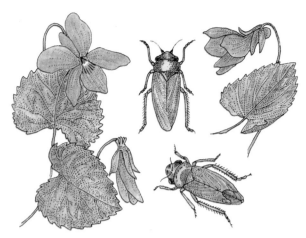

Violets and leaf hoppers who feed on sap.

Red clover and a bumble bee. Bumble bees make their nests in the ground, or in dense vegetation, where they live in colonies.

Dandelion

Many species of beetle rely on plants and trees for food. Some species feed on flowers or leaves or fruit, while others eat nectar and pollen. Some species of beetle prefer to eat caterpillars or small insects such as mites, aphids and scale insects.

A solitary bee visits the flowers of greater stitchwort and white clover. The bee mixes nectar and pollen to make pellets. She puts them into her burrow-like nest as food for her larvae.

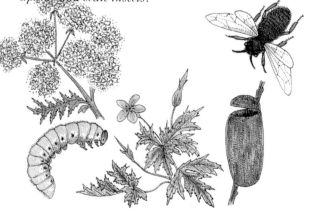

Sawfly larva, cocoon and adult sawfly with cow-parsley and herb-Robert. Sawfly larvae resemble the caterpillars of butterflies and moths.

The illustrations on these two pages show a small selection of the wild flowers which are often found growing in the hedges and of the insects that visit them.

Buttercup

Snipe fly and common mallow. Male snipe flies sit on leaves where they lie in wait for unsuspecting prey. Their larvae hunt in leaf litter.

Some beetles attach their eggs to leaves or twigs while others leave their eggs on tree bark, where the larva will later feed.

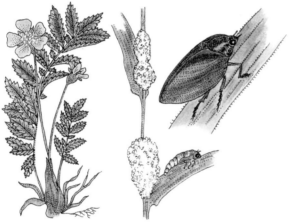

Silverweed and frog-hopper. Frog-hoppers are bugs who live by sucking plant sap. The nymphs develop in a frothy secretion known as cuckoo spit.

Ladybirds and wood anemones. The yellow and black 22-spot ladybird (i) feeds mainly on mildews. The red and black two-spot ladybird (ii) and its larva feed on aphids.

The flowers attract the insects that are preyed on by birds. Too often the delicate balance of nature is destroyed by the use of harsh herbicides and pesticides.

Comfrey and honey bees. If the bee's tongue isn't long enough to reach the nectar, the insect chews a hole at the base of the flower and sips it instead.

A HEDGE

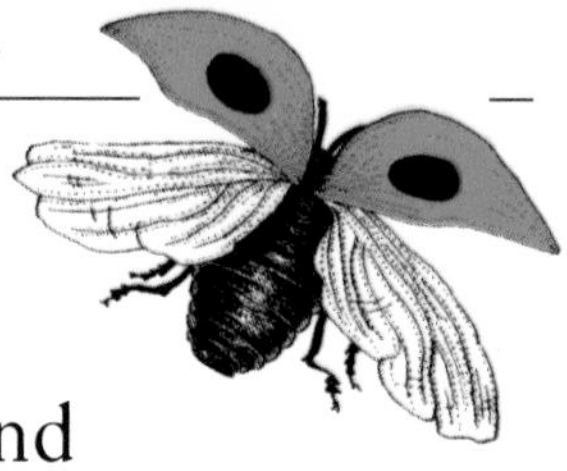

When you walk past a hedge, you may not see the insects and spiders who live there. So stand quietly and watch; as your eyes become adjusted to the shapes and shadows, you will probably be surprised at what you see on bark, leaves, stems and flowers.

WHO INHABITS THE HEDGE?

Lay a piece of white material on the ground under a bush, then shake a branch hard. With luck you will dislodge some insects and spiders on to the cloth. Many of the insects you will find are colored to merge in with the background of their habitat—they will be brown, gray or green. Some will be red and black or yellow and black; these are warning colors to tell predators either that the insect tastes bad or that it stings. There are also some harmless insects who display false warning colors to escape being eaten and there are some flies who mimic wasps or bees.

Ladybirds are predators, eating many plant pests. They are not eaten by birds.

When you have had a good look at the insects you found, and may have been able to identify some of them, put them back gently under the hedge to continue their lives.

The picture opposite shows a portion of a hedge and some of the animals you may find around it. How many can you find?

SNAILS AND EARTHWORMS

Slugs and snails belong to a class of animals called gastropods, meaning 'stomach foot'. Their stomach acts as a foot, easing their body along on a film of slime.

the radula in action

 OBSERVING POND SNAILS

Put some gravel, a water plant and some water that has been standing all night, into a large jar or small tank. Put the snails in the water.

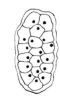

water-snail eggs

Watch the bands of muscle ripple along the snail's body as it moves. See how it eats algae from the glass by rasping with its radula—the tongue like strip in its mouth.

How does the snail breathe? How often does it fill its lungs? When it lays eggs, how long does it take for them to hatch? (You will find some answers on page 75.) Remember to put the snails back into a pond when you have finished observing them. *look for the breathing aperture*

OBSERVING EARTHWORMS

The burrowing of earthworms is important to the fertility of the soil. To watch them in action, fill a small tank or a large glass or plastic jar with alternating layers of garden soil, sand and peat. Scatter some leaves on the top and introduce a few earthworms. Screen the sides of your wormery so that light does not disturb the worms.

Keep the top of the soil damp (but not wet). Look every day to see how the animals mix up the materials. Are they using the leaves? Put the worms back in the garden when you have seen how they work.

AUTUMN

As summer draws to a close, the leaves of the trees begin to change color. Elms and sycamores become tinged with yellow; bracken turns bronze; while blackberry and sloe fruits ripen.

Early autumn brings warm sunny days but longer, cooler nights; the sharp drop in temperature causes morning mists to roll over the countryside and heavy dew to spangle cobwebs and grass blades. On still, clear nights there is frost.

The roots of trees and shrubs find it hard to take water from the cold ground, so plants must shed leaves in order to cut down the amount of water they need. The stem of each leaf is sealed off by a layer of special cells, and the leaves change color and die. So the greens of summer gradually give way to the golds, browns and reds of dying leaves, nuts and juicy berries. Red admiral butterflies sip the juice of fallen pears and of blackberries; wasps feed on split plums; small mammals and birds feast on apples.

There are very few flying insects left and the birds who migrated from Tropical America to feed on them have gradually been leaving, retracing their long journey to overwinter in the sun. Swallows are among the last migrants to go, gathering in chattering flocks on telephone wires before they, too, fly away.

Field mice gather up rose-hips, hawthorn berries, nuts and seeds, which they store in empty birds' nests; squirrels and jays make secret food stores which they will try to find again on cold winter days. Hibernating animals find snug resting-places where fallen leaves make a warm blanket; ladybirds cluster in cracks—nature prepares for winter.

SEED DISPERSAL

Like animals, plants need to spread to new areas in order to find a space to grow away from the parent plant, but as they are rooted to the ground it is their fruits and seeds that have to travel. Apples, hazelnuts, rose-hips, hawthorn berries and blackberries are only a few of the many fruits that protect the seeds they contain until these are carried away by animals, blown by the wind or moved by water to a place where a new plant can take root and grow. The scattering of seeds is called dispersal and the various ways in which this mechanism takes place are illustrated on these two pages.

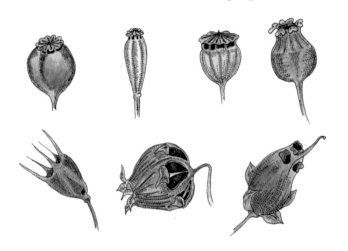

Some plants rely on the wind shaking their seeds out from a capsule, which bursts when it is ripe. Poppies, campion, harebell, campanula and snapdragon belong to this group.

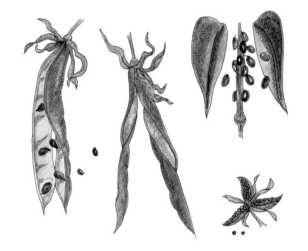

Some dry-fruited plants have explosive pods which fling the seeds away from the parent plant. Lupin, shepherd's purse and pansy all disperse seeds in this way.

Water disperses some fruits and seeds that are kept afloat by corky or spongy outgrowths. Waterlily, marsh cinquefoil, alder and marsh bedstraw have seeds dispersed by water.

Some seeds have special hooks or spines which catch in fur, wool or clothes, so that animals and people disperse them. Here are avens, hound's tongue, bur-marigold and cleavers.

44

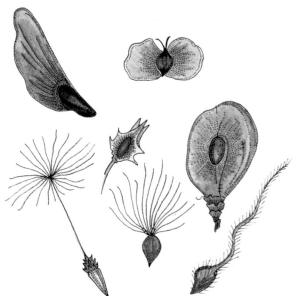

Many fruits are carried away by wind. Look for sail-like outgrowths on the seeds of pine and on the winged fruits of birch, elm and dock. Dandelion, willowherb and clematis seeds have silky "parachutes."

Succulent fruits such as blackberries, hawthorn berries, rose-hips, strawberries, apples and holly berries are eaten by birds and mammals who discard the seeds far from the parent plant.

American goldfinches visit teasel plants, scattering seeds as they pull at the fruits.

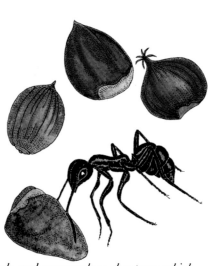

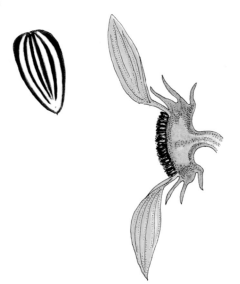

Nut-eating birds and mammals make stores which they may not find again. Bluejays disperse chestnuts, acorns and hazelnuts, while ants harvest gorse seeds to tap for oil.

House finches feast on sunflower seeds. Sunflowers are easy to grow from seed. Sow the seeds in spring and watch them grow. The seed case protects the plant's first leaves until they are well above the soil.

THE SPIDER'S WEB

Garden **spiders** make beautiful webs in which to catch
the small **insects** they prey on. Try to capture a web
on a piece of card. You will have to be very patient,
as you may get the first web or two tangled.

 CAPTURE A WEB

You will need:
a piece of white or colored cardboard or stiff paper
   big enough to hold your chosen web
paper glue or spray mount
an empty non-gas-based spray container
diluted poster paint or powder paint
scissors
a sheet of acetate (optional)

First make sure the spider is not on the web.

Spray the web lightly with the coloring:
if you spray too hard the web will break.

Spread a thin film of glue on to the cardboard.

Bring the sticky side of the cardboard carefully up behind
the web, then bring the cardboard toward you. Try to get all the web
on to the cardboard at the same time.

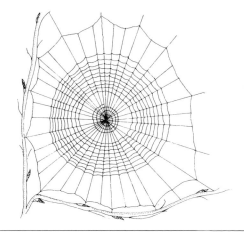

paint

Spray well away from the web

When you have made your catch, cut the supporting strands of the web.

To keep your trophy safe and clean, you may wish to cover it with a sheet of transparent acetate. The glue on the card will hold the acetate in place.

If you go back to where you captured the web, you may be able to watch the spider spin another web. How long does this take?

Count the number of spokes there are stretching from the hub in the center of the web to the strand that goes around the outside. How many circuits go round the inside of the web?

Spinning a web

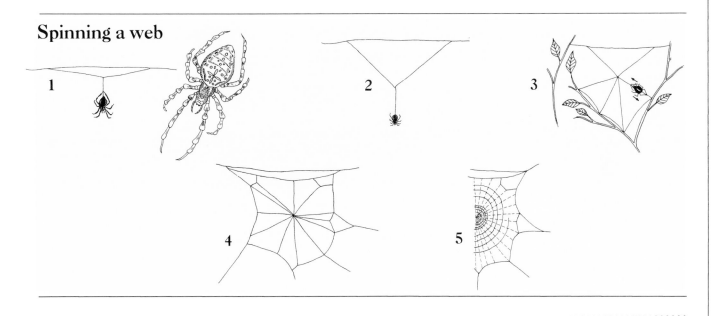

GLOSSARY   **Spider:** a spider has eight legs (four pairs) for walking and a pair of short palps that work like hands. There is no larva or pupa stage in the life of a spider.

Insect: an insect has six legs (three pairs) and a pair of antennae—"feelers". An insect's boy is divided into three parts—head, thorax and abdomen—and most insects have wings. An insect's life normally consists of four stages: egg; larva—the feeding and growing stage; pupa—the resting and changing stage; and finally imago—the full-sized insect.

GALL SPOTTING

As you walk in a park or in the woods looking at the trees, shrubs and **herbaceous** plants, you may see unusual growths or swellings which sometimes resemble fruits. These growths are known as galls and are usually caused by tiny **parasites** growing inside the plant.

When we are stung by a wasp, our bodies respond by swelling up in the area of the sting; when tiny insects, **mites** or **bacteria** irritate the **cells** of a plant, the plant responds by producing a gall. Different types of galls are illustrated on pages 49 and 50. Galls are usually pale green to begin with, but often turn red in summer and brown or black in winter. Cut an oak-apple gall and see how many larval chambers are inside. The majority of the insect species who cause these galls are generally referred to as gall wasps. There are over 700 species of gall wasps in North America alone.

★ THINGS TO DO

Keep a few galls in a jar and see what happens. (Pink oak-apple galls, collected at midsummer, work very well.) Put a layer of dry sand at the bottom of the jar – this will absorb excess moisture. Place the galls on the sand and cover the top of the jar with fine muslin, so that the air can circulate. Keep the jar out of direct sunlight and spray the galls lightly every week with tepid water to prevent them from drying out. As the gall-causers bore their way out, you will see just what they look like.

GLOSSARY   **Herbaceous plant:** a plant that is not woody.
Parasite: an animal or plant that lives in or on another, from which it takes food.
Mite: a minute member of the spider group.
Bacteria: tiny single-celled organisms that cause decay in plants and disease in animals and people.
Cell: a microscopic unit in a living body; plants and animals are made up of millions of cells.

Oak-apple galls are caused by wingless female gall wasps who lay eggs at the base of oak leaf buds in spring. Each gall has a number of chambers from which winged males and females emerge in summer. After mating, the females burrow into the soil and lay eggs in the fine rootlets of the oak, causing brown root galls to develop.

Cherry galls are ¾ inch in diameter. They contain a female gall wasp larva. In winter, the females escape from the galls and lay eggs in dormant oak buds. Males and females emerge from the galls in June and, after mating, eggs are laid in the leaves.

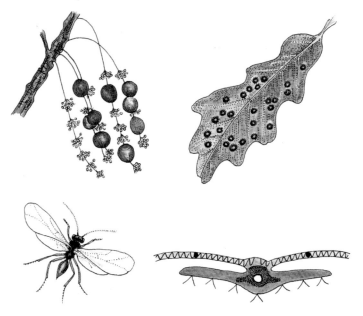

Spangle galls are caused by mated female gall wasps. The galls fall to the ground when they mature in autumn, and over-winter blanketed by fallen leaves. In spring, female gall wasps emerge to lay eggs among the male oak flowers, causing "currant" galls to develop.

Oak-marble galls are caused in the developing leaf buds by another species of gall wasp. Each gall contains a single larva and the gall wasps that emerge are all female.

more to come on page 50

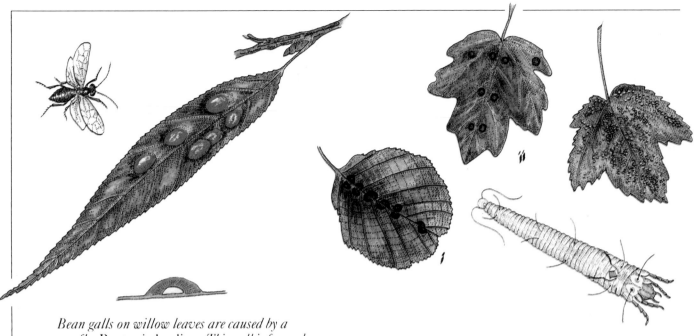

Bean galls on willow leaves are caused by a sawfly, Pontania hyalina. This gall is formed as a reaction to a substance injected by the sawfly when it lays its egg into the leaf.

These galls are caused by tiny Eriophyid mites on (i) alder, (ii) maple, and on many other trees, such as birch, elms, dogwood, and cherry.
(i) The brown galls on the alder mature in autumn.
(ii) The red-brown galls on the maple mature in autumn.

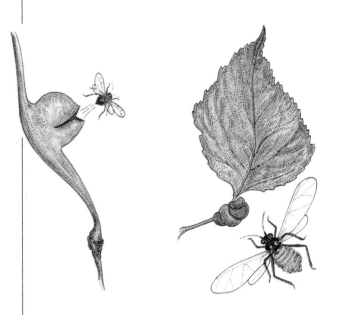

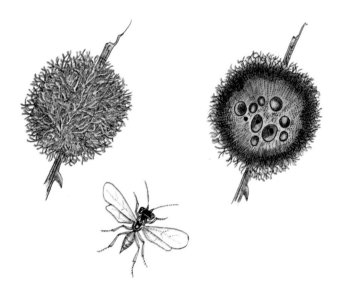

Purse galls on the leaf stalks of Lombardy poplar are caused by an aphid. Spiral galls, also found on the leaf stalks of Lombardy poplar, are caused by another species of aphid. Both types of gall appear in spring when a newly hatched female becomes enclosed in developing cells and reproduces there.

Mossy rose galls can be found on the stems of wild roses. There may be up to sixty chambers inside one fuzzy red gall. Each chamber contains a larva of the gall wasp Diplolepsis rosae. The galls mature in autumn.

LEAVES IN AUTUMN

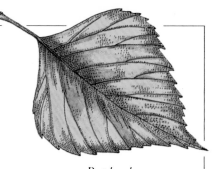

*Poplar leaves
are deciduous.*

Autumn leaves are easy to collect and carry home.
You can press them, take prints of them or
make a collage using a number of leaves.

The leaves shown on pages 52 and 53 are all from deciduous
trees. These are trees that shed their leaves in autumn.

In autumn, chlorophyll, the compound that gives leaves their
green color, is prevented from being produced when a corky layer
begins to form between each leaf and the twig it hangs from. The
leaves then change color from green to beautiful shades of
yellow, gold, orange and red; these colors are produced by the
chemicals that remain in the leaf when the chlorophyll has gone.
Eventually the wind, rain or frost causes the leaf to fall.

Trees that do not shed their leaves in autumn are
called evergreen trees. Evergreen conifers
(cone-bearing trees) have tiny, needle-shaped leaves
with thick, waterproof skins. Holly and other
broad-leaved trees have tough leaves with thick,
waxy, protective skins.

*Pine trees and holly (on the right)
are evergreen.*

Next time you go for a walk in the park or the
countryside, feel the difference between a
deciduous leaf and an evergreen leaf. Take
the deciduous leaf in one hand and the
evergreen leaf in the other. You will see
that the deciduous leaf is thin and matt and
the evergreen leaf is thick and shiny.

51

Collecting autumn leaves is a good way to learn to identify the trees they belong to, but remember that autumn leaves blow about in the wind, so they are not always found beneath the tree they fell from.

willow

Leafless trees can also be identified by their shape against the sky. However, the situation in which a tree grows will affect its general shape. Does the tree you are observing grow in a sheltered place or is it windswept? Is it close to a building or other trees? Can you think how these factors might affect the shape and height of the tree?

hawthorn

If you enjoy collecting and drying autumn leaves, there are many ways in which you can keep them. Do not press leaves inside a book, as the pages will be stained or damaged. The best way is to arrange the leaves on one side of an open newspaper laid out flat. When the leaves are all in position, close the newspaper and cover it with a pile of heavy books or a board. In a few days, the leaves will be dry and flat and ready to use.

MAKING PICTURES FROM FALLEN LEAVES

These two projects are messy activities, so put plenty of newspaper on the table or the floor.

✦ LEAF OUTLINES ✦

You will need:
dry, hard autumn leaves that have fallen from the trees
a few sheets of thin white cardboard or thick paper
an empty non-gas spray container
double-stick tape
several sheets of newspaper

sycamore

Choose a leaf and use small pieces of double-stick to fix it into the desired position on the paper or card.

With plenty of paint on your paintbrush, paint over all the edges of the leaf and on to the paper. Wait until the paint is dry before picking the leaf up carefully. You will have an exact outline of the leaf on the paper. In this way you can record the leaf shapes of all the trees in your area.

chestnut

hophornbeam

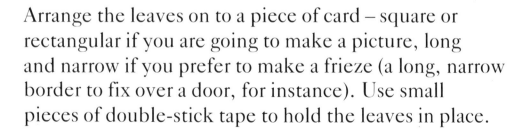

oak

✦ LEAF STENCILS ✦

You will need:
   dry, hard autumn leaves that have fallen from the trees
   a few sheets of white card or thick paper
   an empty non-gas spray container
   diluted poster paint or powder paint
   double-stick tape
   several sheets of newspaper

board

hazel

Arrange the leaves on to a piece of card – square or rectangular if you are going to make a picture, long and narrow if you prefer to make a frieze (a long, narrow border to fix over a door, for instance). Use small pieces of double-stick tape to hold the leaves in place.

lime or linden

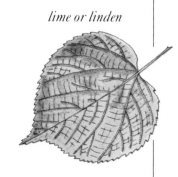

Spread the sheets of newspaper out over the table or the floor and put your prepared picture or frieze on to them.

Now spray paint evenly over the leaves and the card background. Keep the spray container at least 18 inches away from the picture.

When the paint is absolutely dry, you can remove the leaves.

DECOMPOSERS

Decomposers are very important members of any **ecosystem**. Undigested food in **excreta** and the dead bodies of plants and animals still contain energy and raw materials; decomposers feed on these, breaking them down into simple raw materials which enter the soil to be used again by plants.

Most decomposers are either bacteria or **fungi**. Bacteria are so small that they can only be seen through a powerful microscope, but they work at breaking down dead plants and animals. Fungi such as mushrooms and toadstools usually break down plant material. This may sound unpleasant, but the decomposers are nature's sanitation department. Without them we would be surrounded by piles of dead material and disease would bring life to a stop.

You can watch some decomposers at work by observing a dead bird or a small mammal that a dog or cat has brought in. Make sure you have an adult's permission to do this.

YOU MUST WEAR RUBBER GLOVES WHEN HANDLING DEAD ANIMALS AND SCRUB YOUR HANDS WELL WHEN YOU HAVE FINISHED.

 ★ DECOMPOSER PROJECT

You will need:
    a pair of rubber gloves (or help from an adult)
    some wire mesh or a piece of fruit net
        or plastic pea netting
    four short pieces of wood to act as pegs
    a notebook and pencil

Put the dead animal into a shady place. Peg the wire mesh or netting over the body (as shown opposite) so that **scavengers** cannot carry the **carrion** away. Look at the body each day and make notes of the visitors who come to it.

Some of the creatures who may come and feed on carrion

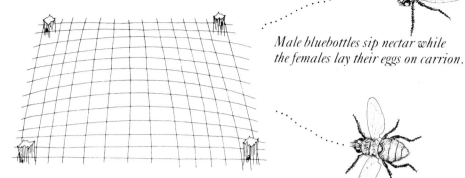

Male bluebottles sip nectar while the females lay their eggs on carrion.

Adult flesh flies sip nectar from flowers; but they mate near a dead animal and their young feed on the rotting flesh.

Put the dead animal under the net.

Greenbottles are interested in smelly garbage cans and carrion; the females lay eggs on the rotting food.

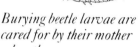

Burying beetle larvae are cared for by their mother when they are young.

Fly larvae are legless and move about by wriggling.

Ground beetles have a beautiful metallic sheen. Both adults and larvae are carnivorous; the adult beetles eat the larvae of other creatures who feed on a dead animal.

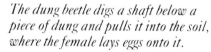

The fine threads of fungi weave their way into and around decaying matter, taking food and helping to break down the dead plant or animal.

The dung beetle digs a shaft below a piece of dung and pulls it into the soil, where the female lays eggs onto it.

GLOSSARY **Ecosystem:** a community of plants and animals living together in a habitat such as a field.
Excreta: waste products from the bodies of animals and man.
Fungi: a group that includes mushrooms, toadstools,
(singular **Fungus**) molds and yeasts.
Scavenger: an animal who feeds on carrion.
Carrion: dead and rotting flesh.

WHAT HAPPENS TO A FALLEN LEAF?

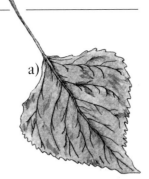
a)

a) Fallen leaves carpet the ground, providing shelter and nesting material for many animals. Even when a leaf has fallen, it contains valuable food reserves which can be returned to the soil and absorbed by the roots of plants.

Let us discover what happens to a fallen leaf.

b) Animals too tiny to see without a magnifying glass begin to eat holes in the leaf. These creatures include tiny mites, springtails, bristletails and minute proturans.

c) Then the even smaller bacteria and fungi start their work; silently, mysteriously, they begin to break down the tough parts of the leaf.

d) As the leaf becomes weaker, more members of the soil and leaf-litter community begin to chew it. Turn some leaf litter over and you may see some of these little animals

d)

scurrying away from the light. There are woodlice, looking like small gray tanks; pill bugs, who roll up into a tight ball; millipedes, with their many short legs; earthworms of various colors and lengths; and the slow-moving slugs and snails. You may also see some of the predators of these animals: the harvestman with its eight long legs, various beetles, shiny brown centipedes and spiders.

e) By this time the leaf is well chewed, and earthworms pull fragments into the soil. After eating the leaf pieces, the earthworms excrete the wastes, which become mixed in with the soil, increasing its richness and making the minerals stored in the leaf available to other plants.

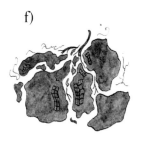

f) The soil is then loosened and well mixed by burrowing animals such as the mole.

Can you make food chains involving the animals you find in the leaf litter? Here is a short one: fallen leaf ➝ worm ➝ mole

★ LOOKING AT THE ANIMALS OF LEAF LITTER

You will need:
 a few handfuls of leaf litter collected in a dry bucket
 a fine sieve
 a large sheet of white paper
 a reading lamp
 a white saucer
 a paintbrush
 a magnifying glass

Put a small amount of leaf litter into the sieve and shake the sieve hard over the white paper. Continue doing this until you have used all your litter. The tiny creatures who inhabit the leaf litter will fall through the sieve on to the paper, along with loose litter. Put the leaves that won't go through the sieve back into the bucket.

Shine the light of the reading lamp on to the paper and use the paintbrush to turn over the sieved litter. The animals who may be among it are shy of the light and will scuttle for cover.

Use the paint-brush to pick up the animals and put them on the saucer, where you can look at them through the magnifying glass.

When you have finished, put the leaf litter and the animals back where you found them.

 ## WOODLICE BEHAVIOR

The flat, gray woodlice who are found in leaf litter can also be found in rotting logs, under large stones or under a pile of old bricks, in the compost heap or under the garbage can. Woodlice eat decaying vegetation, fungi and wood, and they need to live in damp conditions as their body covering is not waterproof and they dry out in open, sunny places.

Here is an experiment that will help you to discover how woodlice behave.

You will need:
a clean, empty margarine container
a seed tray
some very dry soil
some cold water
an old newspaper
a magnifying glass

Collect a few woodlice in the margarine pot. Put the dry soil into the seed tray and water ONE HALF of the tray well. Carefully place half of your woodlouse collection on the dry half of the soil and the other half on the damp half. Cover the whole seed tray with a newspaper and leave it for a few minutes. Have all the woodlice gone to the dry side or the damp side of the soil?

Now wet the dry side of the soil too and cover ONLY this side with the newspaper. What do the woodlice do now?

Look at a woodlouse through a magnifying glass.

Female woodlice do not lay their eggs and leave them hidden; instead they keep them in pockets underneath their body, where the young hatch. Look at woodlice from time to time during the year, and one day you will find one with a litter of tiny white babies hanging on underneath their mother's body.

Put the woodlice back into their habitat.

Some of the decomposers you find in leaf litter may also be found in a compost heap. Take your magnifying glass and see what you can see. Even if you can't SEE anything, the warmth you feel in the center of a compost heap tells you the bacteria are at work.

Springtails, proturans and pauropods are all very small soil animals.

Beetle larvae and snails wander through the loose leaves.

Bumblebees often make their nests in compost heaps, and slugs lay their eggs there, too; both are taking advantage of the warmth.

MUSHROOMS AND TOADSTOOLS

Fungi are unable to make their own food because they do not contain the chemical chlorophyll. Chlorophyll is the cause of the green color in most plants and helps them to turn carbon dioxide, water and minerals into food for their own use, and to release oxygen into the atmosphere.

If you walk in a wood or park in autumn you will see fungi of all sorts; they seem to appear mysteriously overnight as if from nowhere. Fungi reproduce by **spores** instead of seeds. The spores are very tiny and air currents carry them to new areas. Let us find out how a mushroom grows.

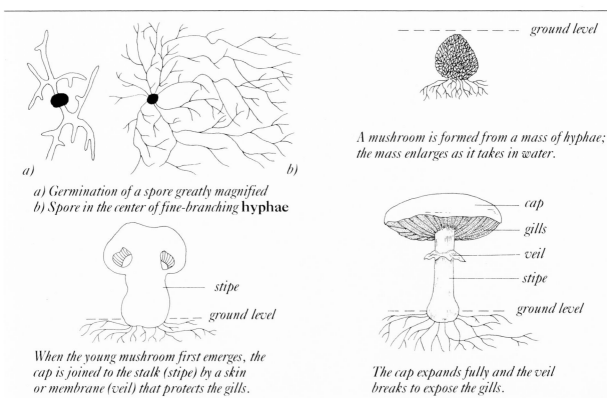

a)

b)

a) Germination of a spore greatly magnified
b) Spore in the center of fine-branching **hyphae**

ground level

A mushroom is formed from a mass of hyphae; the mass enlarges as it takes in water.

stipe

ground level

cap

gills

veil

stipe

ground level

When the young mushroom first emerges, the cap is joined to the stalk (stipe) by a skin or membrane (veil) that protects the gills.

The cap expands fully and the veil breaks to expose the gills.

GLOSSARY   **Spore:** a tiny reproductive body, able to grow into a new plant. Ferns, mosses and fungi have spores, while flowering plants have seeds.
Hyphae: fine threads that are the growing and feeding (singular **hypha**) part of a fungus.

WINTER

Winter is the season of short days and long, cold nights; a time when the processes of life continue, but at a much slower pace.

It is a harsh time of year when there may be snowfalls, heavy rain, high winds, fog or frost, all mixed in with the occasional mild day. Food is scarce and the time for finding it is short; mammals and birds use up a lot of energy simply keeping warm. In autumn animals eat well to build up a good layer of fat under the skin, and it is often these reserves of fat that keep them alive through the winter. Only the fit and strong will see spring.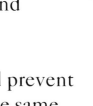

We wear clothes in order to trap air next to our skin and prevent our bodies from losing heat; fur and feathers work in the same way for animals.

Some animals change color in winter so that they merge with their habitat. In parts of the country where snow is common in winter, weasels become white. Snowshoe hares have a white winter coat, and ptarmigan grow white feathers, while wading birds have a dull brown or gray plumage in winter. You may like to find out about other animals that change color in winter.

Some animals try to escape winter by sleeping through it; this is called hibernation. Chipmunks are true hibernators; they go to sleep in early autumn and do not wake up until spring is well under way. Bats only wake up in winter if there is a spell of mild weather. Several mammals, including squirrels, stay in their nests during really bad weather, but they have to look for food every few days if they are not to starve. NEVER disturb a hibernating animal.

NATURE DETECTIVE 1—ANIMAL TRACKS

Animal tracks are easiest to see when a little fine snow has fallen on the hard surface of a road, on a path in the park, or around your house. Look for tracks on soft ground after heavy rain, on the muddy earth around a pond, by a river, or in the wet sand of a beach at low tide. Estuaries and mud-flats will have many bird tracks but be very careful in these habitats: DO NOT GET CUT OFF BY THE TIDE and DO NOT WADE INTO THE MUD as you may become stuck and sink in. Go with an adult.

Take a notebook, pencil and ruler with you to measure and record any track you find. Measure the length of the footprint, from the back edge of the pad to the front edge of the longest toe. Do not include the claws in the measurement. Then measure the width of the footprint at its widest part. Even better, take some sheets of clear plastic and a waterproof felt-tip pen with you; when you find a track, put one of the plastic sheets over it and trace over the outline of the footmark.

Rabbits and hares have similar tracks, but the rabbit's are smaller. Use an empty matchbox to test the difference. If the width of the hindfoot track is about the same width as the matchbox, the track was made by a hare; if the track is only about two-thirds of the width of the box, then it is a rabbit track. Here the forefoot is shown on the left, the hindfoot on the right.

This is the hind print of a badger. It is about 1 inch wide; 2 inches long to the back edge of the main pad and 2½ inches to the heel – the dotted line. The print of the forefoot would show five long, strong claws.

The toes of a red fox are grouped closely together. In winter, look for traces of hair between the pads and the toes. The fifth toe of the forefoot is placed so high that it doesn't leave a mark. The foot is about 2 inches long and 1½ inches wide.

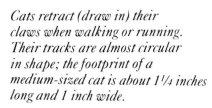

Cats retract (draw in) their claws when walking or running. Their tracks are almost circular in shape; the footprint of a medium-sized cat is about 1¼ inches long and 1 inch wide.

Dog tracks vary in size. The toes radiate outwards. Compare these tracks to those of a fox.

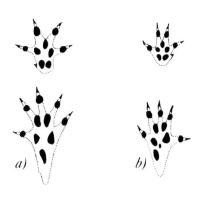

a) Deer mouse tracks. The forefoot is ¼ inch long and the hindfoot ¾ inch long.

b) Vole tracks. The forefoot is ½ inch long and the hindfoot 1 inch long.

    The width of each depends on how splayed the toes are at the time, and this will vary with the terrain.

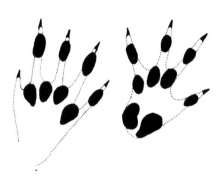

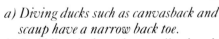

Gray and red squirrels have four toes on the forefeet and five on the hindfeet. The claws show very clearly. The forefoot track is about 1½ inches long and ¾ inch wide, the hindfoot about 2 inches long and 1 inch wide.

a) Pigeon tracks are ½ inch long and can be found in towns, parks, gardens, fields and woodlands.

b) Sparrow tracks are ¾ inch long.

a) Diving ducks such as canvasback and scaup have a narrow back toe.

b) Dabbling ducks such as mallard and teal have a round back toe. The middle toe of the mallard is about 2 inches long.

Swan and goose tracks are similar in shape, but the goose's foot is smaller. Swan tracks are about 6¼ inches long.

A pheasant track is about 2¾ inches long; you can often see the mark left by its long tail in the snow.

Draw diagrams of any footprint patterns you find. Do you think the animal was walking, trotting or running? The faster the movement, the greater the gap between the sets of tracks.

It is fun to try making plaster casts of the animal tracks you find. Snow, soft mud or sand show good tracks which you will be able to identify, but they do not make good casts, as they will melt or collapse. Look for good clear tracks that are free from water, on the soft soil of a woodland path, in an unpaved garden or park pathway, or in the firm mud beside a pond.

You will need:
plaster of Paris
some cold water in a plastic bottle
an old spoon
a plastic bowl
some strips of thin cardboard about
    12 inches long and 2 inches wide

a few paper clips
a newspaper
a trowel
an old nail-brush or toothbrush

Find a good clear track and move any leaves and stones out of the way. Bend one of the strips of card around to enclose the track; fasten the ends together with a paper clip and press the cardboard ring down a little so that it is able to stand firmly in the soil or mud around the print.

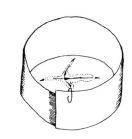

You will need to mix enough plaster of Paris to fill the depression made by the animal's foot and to form a layer about 1 inch deep above it. When you have practiced on a few tracks you will know how much plaster of Paris powder you need for each cast.

Mix the plaster of Paris by putting some of the powder into the bowl and adding water, a little at a time, stirring all the while with the spoon. When the mixture feels and looks like thick cream, pour it slowly and carefully into the card ring to prevent air pockets from forming; make sure that it fills the track and goes to the edge of the ring. Smooth the surface with the spoon.

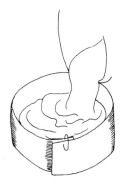

Use newspaper to clean the bowl and spoon straight away, or the plaster will dry hard and will be difficult to remove. Collect all the newspaper to take home with you, DO NOT leave it behind to create litter. The plaster of Paris takes about half an hour to set, but the weather and the thickness of the plaster will affect drying time. If in doubt, wait a little longer. Start looking around for other tracks and trails while you are waiting.

When the plaster has hardened, do not try to remove the cardboard from around the cast but use the trowel to lift the whole thing out of the ground. Wrap it in newspaper to carry it home.

When you reach home, remove the strips of cardboard and turn the cast over so that the track is on the top; carefully brush out the mud using an old nail-brush or toothbrush. Hold the cast under the tap and allow a gentle stream of cold water to wash the mud from the track. Leave the cast to dry.

You can now see the track in all its details; it will be in relief—standing out from the background. You could paint the raised cast to make it show up well. Try dabbing it carefully on to paper, before the paint has dried, to make prints. Add more paint if necessary. Alternatively, you could paint the plaster *around* the cast—this is another way of making the track stand out from its background. If you prefer to keep it white, you could cover it all over with clear varnish (use a paintbrush) which will protect your work from dirt and scratches.

Try pressing the cast into soft plasticine or modeling clay to make a true likeness of the original footprint.

You could make a collection of animal tracks. Don't forget to label them all, recording the identity of the animal, the location and the date at which you made your find. Go back a while later to see if you can see similar tracks.

NATURE DETECTIVE 2–ANIMAL TRAILS

Look for clues to the wildlife that may be living in your area. You may find the remains of food in woods, fields, parks or gardens; these can tell you a great deal. Droppings, too, can tell you a lot about an animal's habits. For example, badgers and cats dig holes to hide their droppings, while foxes and rabbits leave theirs somewhere obvious to mark their territories. Look for entrance holes to underground homes. Who lives there? Look at different birds' nests and see how they are made. Can you make a nest using twigs and grass? Remember, we have nimble fingers, but a bird uses only its beak.

A squirrel begins at the base of a cone and strips off the scales to get at the seeds. A squirrel often has a favourite feeding place where there may be many stripped cones.

Young squirrels leave many teethmarks on nut shells. Older squirrels have more experience and so leave only a few short teethmarks on top of the shell.

A mouse holds the nut at an angle away from its body. Only the bottom teeth gnaw the kernel; the top teeth hold the shell in place. While gnawing, the mouse continually turns the nut around and enlarges the hole, leaving teethmarks on the shell.

A vole has short legs and so holds a nut with its base on the ground, close to its hindfeet. After gnawing a hole in the shell, the vole puts its nose and mouth inside to eat the kernel. This means that there are no teethmarks on the outside and the edge of the hole is neat and even.

You may find many broken snail shells around a rock or tree stump. This is a thrush's anvil. The bird picks up a snail in its beak and hammers it until it breaks.

The bill of a crossbill is well adapted for opening cones. The bird's strong bill pries the scales apart and its sticky tongue takes up the seeds.

The woodpecker wedges a cone into a tree crevice, tip upwards. It hammers at the cone, splitting the scales, then picks out the seeds with its long, sticky tongue.

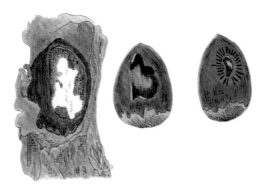

Woodpeckers and nuthatches wedge nuts into crevices and hammer at the shell until it breaks. Tits often eat nuts as they hang on the tree, leaving beak marks on the shell.

Leaf miners are the larvae of tiny moths. Their white **serpentine** mines are very narrow at first, broadening out as the larva, feeding on the leaf tissue, becomes fatter.

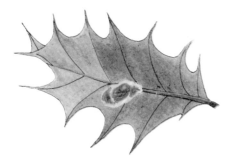

Blotch mines are often made by fly larvae. Look for the escape hole in the brown patch of leaf tissue.

REMEMBER TO WASH YOUR HANDS AFTER HANDLING ANY SPECIMEN

FURTHER CLUES

Look for fur, wool or hairs caught on wooden fences or barbed wire. You may see mushrooms with their caps marked with many closely packed grooves – these are the teethmarks of a small rodent. Mushrooms with shallow depressions in their caps may have been nibbled at by slugs. These don't leave teethmarks!

quill feather *contour feather* *down feather*

Make a collection of feathers and try to find out which bird they came from. Quill feathers are strong and are used in flight. Contour feathers give the bird its shape, while down feathers insulate the body.

OWL PELLETS

An owl may catch three or four small mammals in one night of hunting, swallowing large amounts of indigestible bones and fur. The material that cannot be digested is compressed and compacted in the bird's gizzard—a thick-walled part of the digestive tract, just above the stomach cavity. When the gizzard is full, the owl coughs the pellet up and out of its beak. This happens once or twice a day, the second pellet being ejected just before the owl flies off on an evening's hunting trip. You can often find pellets on the ground underneath an owl's roosting place. They are black and soft when they are fresh, and gray and dry when old.

Owls, magpies, ravens, crows, kestrels, accipiters, gulls and herons are among the birds who **regurgitate** the food they cannot digest in compressed pellets. The pellets may contain fur, feathers, bones, **chitin**, shell from snails or the indigestible parts of plants.

A long-eared owl pellet (about 2-2¾ inches long)

A screech owl pellet (about 1 inch long)

Barn owl pellet (about 1¼ inches in diameter)

The pellet of a horned owl (about 2 inches long)

A short-eared owl pellet. The contents usually consist of the remains of voles.

★ THE OWL'S MEAL

Take a pellet to pieces to see what the bird has been eating.

First, make a drawing of the shape of the pellet and take its measurements. Soak the pellet in warm water overnight, by which time it should be soft enough to dissect. Put the soft pellet into a shallow dish with some clean water. Use a pair of tweezers to pick the tiny bones and teeth out gently—they are easily broken. The bones can be dried and mounted on stiff cardboard. Are there any shiny wing-cases of beetles?

GLOSSARY   **Serpentine:** coiling or winding like a snake.
Regurgitate: to cough out food that cannot be digested.
Chitin: the tough material that forms the outer shell of an insect.

THE LIFE-CYCLE OF A SCOTCH PINE

Conifer trees have **needles** or scalelike leaves. Their foliage
is usually evergreen, a common exception being larch trees. Conifers'
fruits are usually woody cones, but juniper and yew have fleshy berries.
Let us look at the life cycle of a common conifer.

Pine needles are found in twos, threes or fives, held together by
a **sheath** at the base. Scotch pine needles are in pairs; each pair
lives about four years before turning brown and falling as a
unit. Can you identify a Scotch pine using the key on page 72?

In spring you will see tiny, pinkish-green globes growing on the
tips of some of the shoots; these are female cones. The male
cones are clusters of golden **pollen** sacs found further back on
the shoot; these wither away when the pollen has been shed.

On a fine day in late spring these sacs release their pollen,
which is carried by the breeze in a search for another Scotch
pine, where the little female cones open their soft scales to
catch the pollen. The scales of the female cones close over the
pollen grains and will not move apart again for two years, when
the seeds are ready to be shed. The captured pollen grains begin
to grow toward the egg cells at the center of the female cone.
They grow very slowly; during the autumn and winter they stop
growing altogether and become **dormant**. In spring growth begins
again and each egg cell is **fertilized** by the male cell carried in
each grain of pollen.

After fertilization, the cone begins to grow very slowly. At
first it is green but as the seeds develop, the surrounding
scales of the cone become brown and woody; when the winged seeds
are ripe, they are released on a dry day and the breeze carries
them away from the parent tree. Many seeds are shed, but only a
few will **germinate**, and even fewer turn into a new tree.

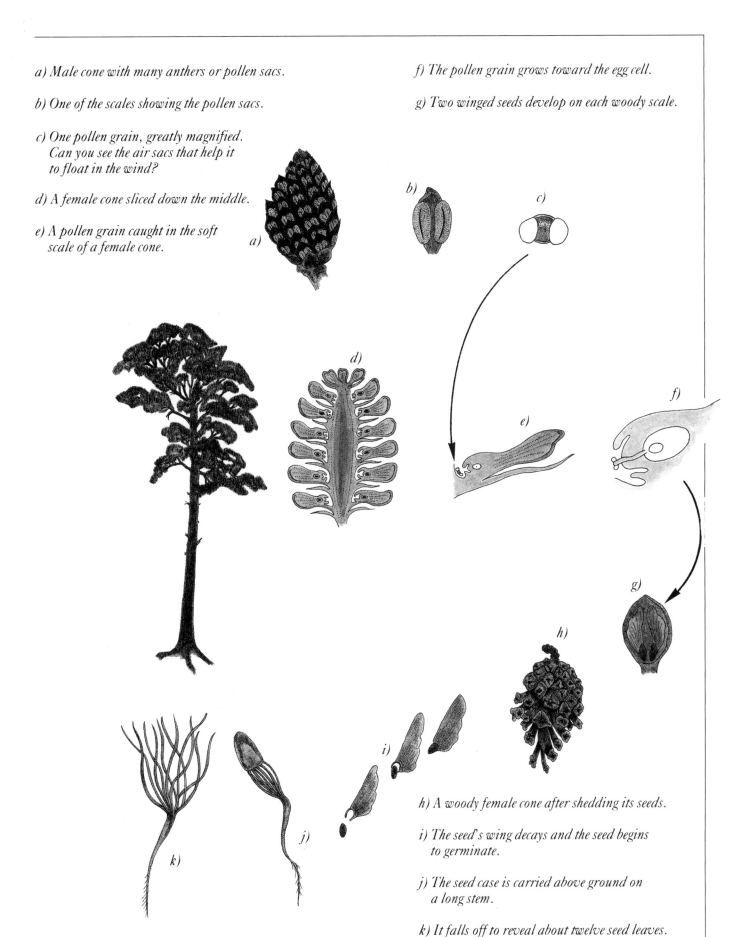

a) *Male cone with many anthers or pollen sacs.*

b) *One of the scales showing the pollen sacs.*

c) *One pollen grain, greatly magnified. Can you see the air sacs that help it to float in the wind?*

d) *A female cone sliced down the middle.*

e) *A pollen grain caught in the soft scale of a female cone.*

f) *The pollen grain grows toward the egg cell.*

g) *Two winged seeds develop on each woody scale.*

h) *A woody female cone after shedding its seeds.*

i) *The seed's wing decays and the seed begins to germinate.*

j) *The seed case is carried above ground on a long stem.*

k) *It falls off to reveal about twelve seed leaves.*

CONIFER KEY

Walk through a park, or a conifer plantation if there is one near you, and try to identify some trees using this simple key.

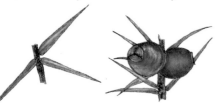

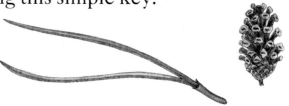

Juniper is a shrub with sharp-pointed, blue-green needles in groups of three, set all around the stem. Look for the purple berries in late autumn.

Pine needles occur in pairs, threes or fives, and are held by a sheath at the base. Scotch pine needles occur in twos.

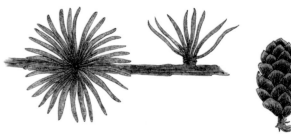

Yew trees are very dark green. In October female trees have soft, scarlet berries; each contains one black seed.

Larch trees are deciduous conifers. The shoots have knobs on them and, when the trees is in leaf, each knob becomes the center of a cluster of 20-30 needles.

Cedars have frond-like foliage—that is, leaves like those of a fern.

Fir needles have a flat, round base and leave a flat, round scar on the stem. Check this by pulling a needle away gently.

Spruce needles are on pegs. When the needle falls naturally, the peg remains; if the needle is pulled, the peg comes too.

Hemlock needles are short and irregular in length. Each needle has two light-colored stripes underneath.

CONES OF ALL SHAPES AND SIZES

Western redcedar

hemlock

Scotch pine

Norway spruce

Monterey cypress

Collect as many different cones as you can and try
to identify them.

Cones open and close their woody scales according
to the dampness in the air. When the air is dry
the scales move apart; when it is damp they close up.
A large cone hung up in a well-ventilated room can be
used as a simple barometer.

Douglas fir

larch

The cones' ability to open and close their scales is a protection
for the ripening seeds. If the ripe cones on the trees were to
open their scales in wet, rainy weather, the seeds would simply
fall to the ground under the parent tree and would not be carried
to a new place to grow. So the cones open when it is dry, and the
seeds have a much greater chance of being scattered by a breeze.

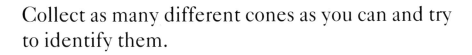

GLOSSARY   **Needles:** name given to the thin, sharp leaves of conifers.
        Sheath: leaf base encasing the stem of a plant.
        Pollen: the powdery grains that flowers produce and
              which carry the male cells necessary for fertilization.
      Dormant: in a sleeplike state.
      Fertilise: to impregnate or make productive—to start a
              seed or a baby growing.
    Germinate: to begin to grow.

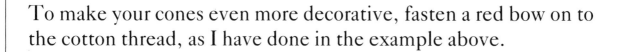

To make very simple decorations, spray or paint cones with gold, silver or white paint. When the paint is dry, you may like to put a little glue on the end of each scale and sprinkle glitter on to the glue.

Tie a length of cotton around the stem at the top of the cone and fasten it into a loop, so that it can hang from the Christmas tree.

You could hang a number of cones from an ivy-covered wire coathanger, varying the lengths of cotton so you have a mobile.

To make your cones even more decorative, fasten a red bow on to the cotton thread, as I have done in the example above.

For cone Christmas dolls, you will need a small piece of red felt and some wooden beads with faces painted on them.

Spray or paint the cones as before. Using glue, fix the bead head on to the stalk that stands up straight at the top of the cone.

While the glue is drying, make the little hat. Measure around the widest part of the bead head and add about ¼ inch: this is the width of the felt you will need. Make the hat about 2 inches high. Fold the felt in two and sew the two sides together to make a tube. Sew all around the top of the tube with little stitches, then pull the thread to close the end up tightly. Fasten off firmly.

Now glue the hat to the bead head. Trim the hat with cotton wool to make it look really festive.

ANSWERS TO QUESTIONS

Page 10: Vegetarian

Page 11: grass → rabbit → weasel
grass → antelope → lion
leaf → slug → toad → fox
leaf → snail → thrush → cat
leaf → worm → hen → man

Page 14: grass → rabbit → weasel
wheat → mouse → kestrel
leaf litter → earthworm → shrew → owl
leaf → caterpillar → small bird → cat
dung → beetle → frog → fox
marine plankton → marine copepod → sand eel → small bird → herring gull

Page 21: On the bottom of the pond, you will find the tubifex worm and the dragonfly nymph. In water of medium depth, near to and among plants, you will find the tadpole and the mayfly nymph. The water snail will be feeding on algae, from stones or from plants. Cyclops, daphnia, the midge larva, and the perch will be swimming freely in water of any depth. The water boatman, water scorpion, and the diving beetle will be near the water surface, where they stick their bottoms out of the water to take in air. The moth larva will be on the pondweed or waterlily leaves.

Page 30: The plants on a wall provide food and shelter for many microscopic invertebrates. Many other creepy-crawlies live inside the wall and they are hunted by shrews; mice and voles patrol the passages too, finding seeds and shelter amongst the stones. Wrens disappear into old walls looking for insect food, while weasels silently stalk the other hunters.

Page 42: The snail comes partly out of the water and takes air into a lunglike cavity under the shell. During the warm days of summer the little snails inside the eggs develop in about two weeks, depending on the water temperature.

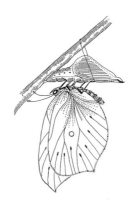

INDEX

Folio numbers printed in *italic* refer to illustrations,
those printed in **bold** refer to entries in the glossary.